Science Biographies

Thomas Edison

Kay Barnham

Raintree

Raintree is an imprint of Capstone Global Library Limited, a company incorporated in England and Wales having its registered office at 7 Pilgrim Street, London, EC4V 6LB – Registered company number: 6695582

www.raintreepublishers.co.uk
myorders@raintreepublishers.co.uk

Text © Capstone Global Library Limited 2014
First published in hardback in 2014
The moral rights of the proprietor have been asserted.

Edited by Dan Nunn, Adam Miller, and Diyan Leake
Designed by Cynthia Akiyoshi
Picture research by Tracy Cummins
Production by Helen McCreath
Originated by Capstone Global Library
Printed and bound in China

ISBN 978 1 406 27244 4
17 16 15 14 13
10 9 8 7 6 5 4 3 2 1

Barnham, Kay
Edison, Thomas. (Science Biographies)
A full catalogue record for this book is available from the British Library.

Acknowledgements
We would like to thank the following for permission to reproduce photographs: Alamy p. 21 (© RGB Ventures LLC dba SuperStock); Corbis pp. 6 (Bettmann), 17 (Library of Congress via Science Faction), 18 (Bettmann); Getty Images pp. 5 (Archive Photos), 7 (Time & Life Pictures), 9 (Keystone-France), 11 (David E. Scherman/Time Life Pictures), 13 (Prisma/UIG), 25 (Hulton Archive), 26 (Science Faction/Library of Congress), 28 (Roger Viollet); From the collections of The Henry Ford p. 27 (THF37936); istockphoto design elements (© James Steidl); Library of Congress Prints and Photographs Division pp. 4, 16, 22, 23; National Archives design elements; NPS Photo p. 12; Science Photo Library p. 10; Shutterstock p. 8 (© Anneka), design elements (© Antonio Abrignani, © Morphart Creation, © Terence Mendoza, © FotoSergio, © Kellis, © Inga Nielsen, © lynea, © Ratana21); Superstock pp. 15 (Dennis MacDonald), 19 bottom (Science Museum/SSPL), 20 (Everett Collection), 24 (Science and Society); Topfoto p. 14 (Topham Picturepoint).

Cover photographs reproduced with permission of Superstock (Stock Montage) and Photo Researchers, Inc. (John M. Daugherty).

Contents

Some words are shown in **bold**, like this. You can find out what they mean by looking in the glossary.

Who was Thomas Edison?

Thomas Edison (1847–1931) was an American inventor. His most famous inventions were the electric light bulb, the **phonograph**, and the **motion picture** camera.

Edison wasn't just an inventor. He was also a businessman. He wanted to invent things that people would buy, so that he would make money. If Edison saw a good idea, he would work hard to make it even better.

Edison famously said that genius is "one per cent inspiration, ninety-nine per cent perspiration".

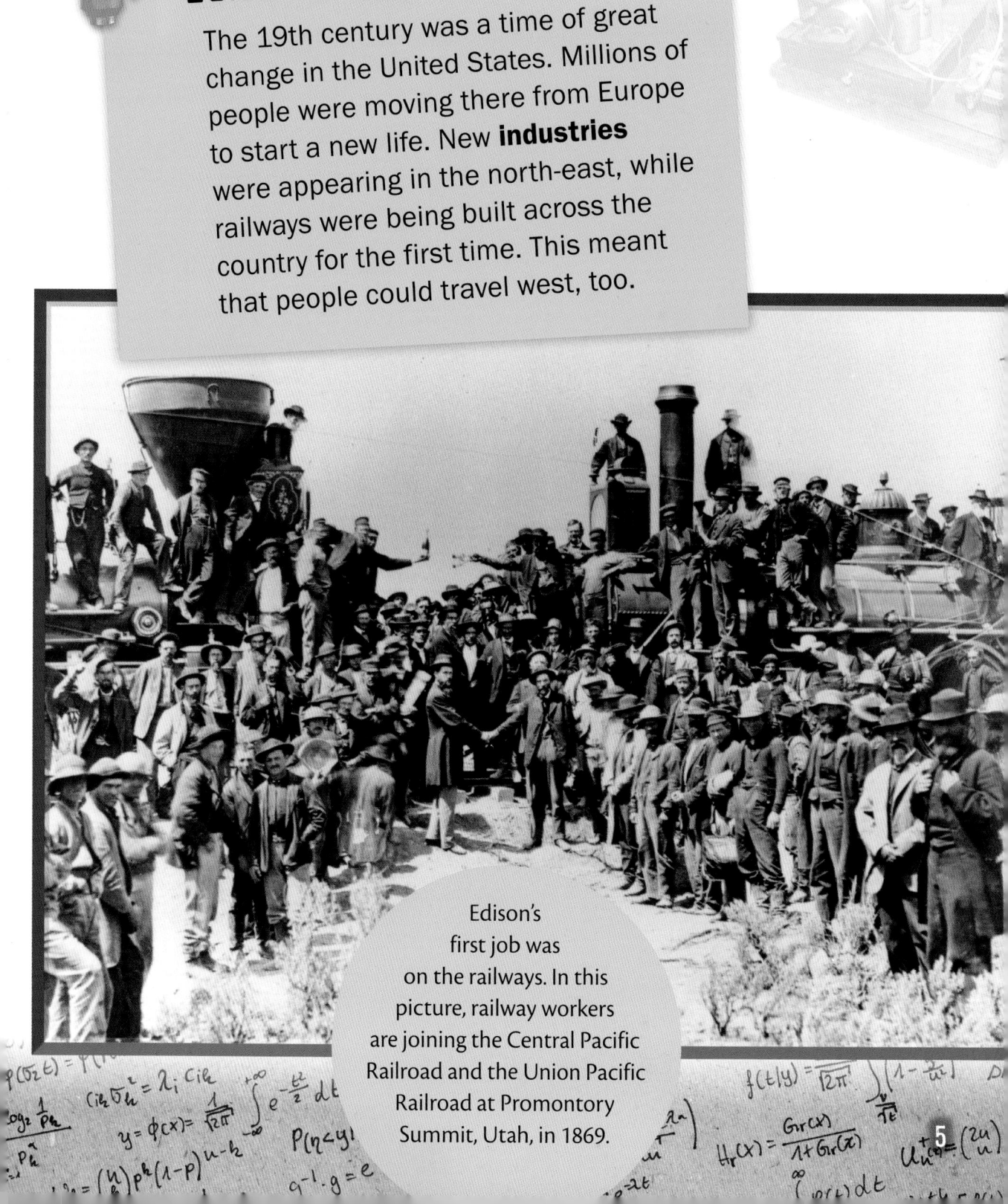

The United States in Edison's day

The 19th century was a time of great change in the United States. Millions of people were moving there from Europe to start a new life. New **industries** were appearing in the north-east, while railways were being built across the country for the first time. This meant that people could travel west, too.

Edison's first job was on the railways. In this picture, railway workers are joining the Central Pacific Railroad and the Union Pacific Railroad at Promontory Summit, Utah, in 1869.

Young Edison

Thomas Alva Edison was born on 11 February 1847 in Milan, Ohio, USA. Al – as his family nicknamed him – was the youngest of seven children.

When Thomas was about eight, he went to school. His teacher couldn't keep up with his questions, so he left after just three months. From then on, Thomas's mother taught him at home. He was always very grateful to his mother for spending so much time teaching him. He wanted to make her proud.

Thomas's favourite subject was science. He loved it so much that he built a **laboratory** for his own experiments.

Thomas was a lively, curious boy who asked lots of questions about how things worked.

Earning money

Thomas was eager to start earning money, and by the age of 12 he had a job. He sold snacks, sweets, and newspapers on the Grand Trunk railway line. Soon, he was printing his own weekly newspaper – the *Grand Trunk Herald* – and selling that, too.

Steam locomotives carried passengers along the Grand Trunk Railroad in Canada and the United States. Thomas worked on the trains that ran between Port Huron and Detroit.

Edison the telegraph operator

In 1862, Thomas saved the life of a little boy who had strayed on to a railway track – and his own life changed forever. The boy's father was a **telegraph** operator. He was so grateful to Thomas that he taught him how to use a telegraph machine. Now, Thomas could get a job as a telegraph operator!

Telegraphy

By the 1860s, telegraphy had become the fastest way of sending messages around the world. Telegraph machines, like this one designed by Samuel Morse, sent messages along a wire using electrical signals. The first long-distance telephone call did not happen until 1915.

Edison travelled around the United States for years, working as a telegraph operator. But he was **ambitious**. He spent his spare time experimenting with new ideas. He loved inventing and hoped that one of his inventions would make his fortune.

Edison sometimes worked night shifts. When he wasn't busy, he could do experiments.

Edison the businessman

In 1869, Edison **patented** his first invention: the electric vote recorder. This machine was designed to save time during elections. Instead of people counting the votes by hand, the machine would do all the hard work. But sales were poor, and Edison was disappointed. He decided that from now he would not "waste time inventing things that people would not want to buy".

What is a patent?

A patent is a **licence** the government gives. It is proof that a person came up with an idea or invention. No one else is allowed to copy the idea, unless they pay a fee to the person who holds the patent.

Edison's vote recorder meant that voters didn't have to fill out voting slips – they simply moved a switch on the **device**.

SUCCESS!

In 1869, Edison left his job and moved to New York City. Here, at last, he started to have some success with his ideas.

Edison invented a new type of **stock ticker** that printed messages in letters and numbers instead of **Morse code**. It meant that traders in **stocks and shares** could get information about prices faster and then make more money.

Thousands of stock tickers were sold. They were used well into the 20th century.

Edison's family

The money Edison made from his stock ticker was enough to open his own business. His employees made and sold telegraph equipment, and there was room for Edison to invent, too.

DOT AND DASH

Mary Stilwell was a worker in Edison's telegraph company. Just two months after she and Edison met, they got married. They had three children together. The first two children were called Marion and Thomas but Edison nicknamed them "Dot" and "Dash" after the short and long signals used in Morse code.

Mary Stilwell married Thomas Edison on Christmas Day 1871. She was 16 years old. He was 24.

More success!

Edison carried on inventing. One of his biggest successes was the quadruplex telegraph machine. It could send not one but *four* messages at the same time!

The quadruplex telegraph transmitter saved telegraph companies a lot of **money** – and made Edison a lot **of money**, too.

The quadruplex telegraph transmitter sent two messages in one direction at the some time that another two messages were being sent in the opposite direction.

The Wizard of Menlo Park

Soon, Edison had a problem. He wanted to employ more people to help him work on his many ideas and inventions, but there just wasn't the space for them in his workshop. He needed more room.

In 1876, the Edison family moved to Menlo Park, New Jersey, where Edison built a research laboratory. He invented so many amazing things here that he became known as the Wizard of Menlo Park.

Edison's research laboratory at Menlo Park was the first of its kind.

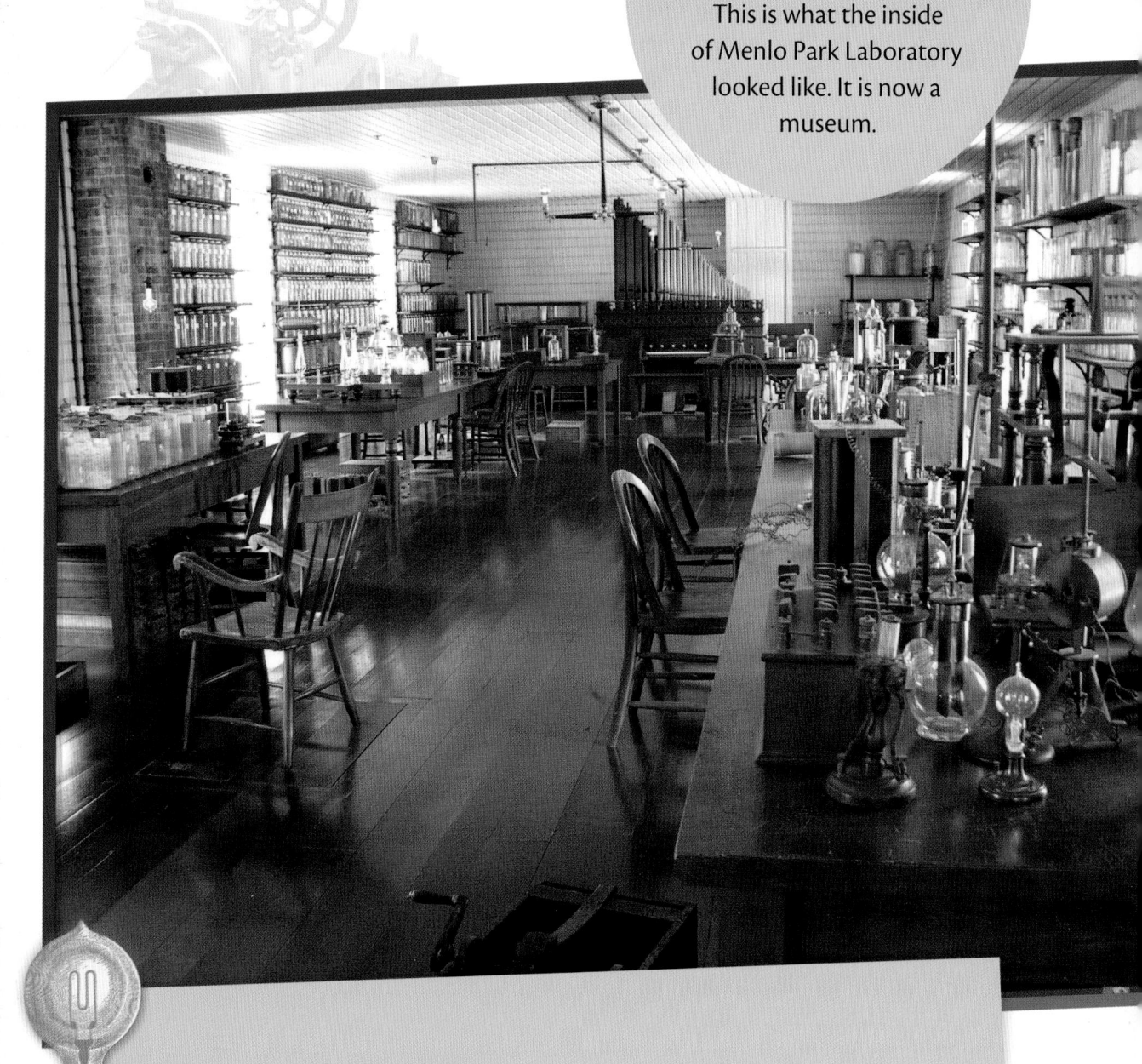

This is what the inside of Menlo Park Laboratory looked like. It is now a museum.

Edison's muckers

Thomas Edison called his laboratory workers "muckers", while he was the "chief mucker". First, Edison had an idea for a device or thought of a way to make something work better. Then, a team of muckers would make and test the idea. Different teams worked on different ideas at the same time, so Edison could invent and patent many ideas at once.

The phonograph

Edison invented the phonograph at Menlo Park. Other inventors had already made machines that recorded sound, but Edison's phonograph did something totally new – it played recorded sound back, too.

As soon as the phonograph was built, Edison recorded his own voice. He said the nursery rhyme "Mary had a little lamb", and was delighted when the phonograph played it right back to him.

This is Thomas Edison and his second version of the phonograph. He came up with the idea while he was trying to find a way to record telephone messages.

This invention of Edison's recorded sound on wax cylinders.

Why were phonographs important?

Phonographs were the first ever way of recording and playing back sound. Edison's early recordings were made on tinfoil sheets, but later they were made on wax cylinders. The next important invention was the gramophone, which played flat, circular, **vinyl** records. Today, music is often recorded **digitally**, but many people still prefer to play vinyl records.

The light bulb

Edison's next great idea was the one for which he is most remembered: the light bulb.

The British scientist Joseph Swan invented the first light bulb to use a carbon filament – a fine thread that glowed when electricity travelled through it. There was a **vacuum** inside the bulb, which meant there was no oxygen inside it. Without oxygen, Swan's light bulb stayed lit. However, the light would only last 13 hours.

Joseph Swan demonstrated his light bulb in 1878, but it didn't glow for very long.

Swan wrote about his ideas in a science magazine so that everyone could read about it. The very next year, Edison patented his own light bulb. It was very similar to Swan's invention.

Edison tried to improve his light bulb. By 1880, it glowed for over 1,200 hours.

Ediswan

Edison and Swan argued over who had invented the light bulb. Finally, in 1883, they formed a company called Ediswan and agreed to work together.

Swan's light bulb (left) had a filament in the shape of a rod. Edison's light bulb (right) had a filament in the shape of a loop. Bending the filament meant that a light bulb would glow for longer.

Light for everyone!

Edison set about making light bulbs that glowed for many hours. He also tried to make them much cheaper so that everyone could buy them. However, light bulbs need electricity to make them work. So the next thing Edison did was to develop a way of supplying electricity to customers, too. In 1882, he opened a power station on Pearl Street in New York City – the first of its kind.

When it opened in 1882, Pearl Street power station generated electricity for just a few hundred light bulbs. Fifty-two of these light bulbs lit the offices of the *New York Times*, a few streets away.

AC versus DC

When electricity was first generated, there were different ways of supplying it to customers. The inventor Nikola Tesla was a big fan of the **alternating current (AC)** system. Meanwhile, Edison thought that **direct current (DC)** was the future. This time Edison was wrong. The AC system is still used today.

Nikola Tesla was a Serbian inventor who had once worked for Edison.

New beginnings

In 1884, Edison's wife Mary died. She was just 29. Edison had already been spending a lot of time away from Menlo Park, working in New York City. Now he moved his children there, too. It was a sad time for all of them.

A year later, Edison and his family visited friends in New England. It was here that he met Mina Miller, the daughter of another inventor.
In 1886, they were married. The family moved to West Orange, New Jersey.

Mina Miller was 20 when she married Edison. He was 39.

Edison's new laboratory in West Orange was built in 1887. It was much bigger than his laboratory at Menlo Park. Half of Edison's inventions would be developed here.

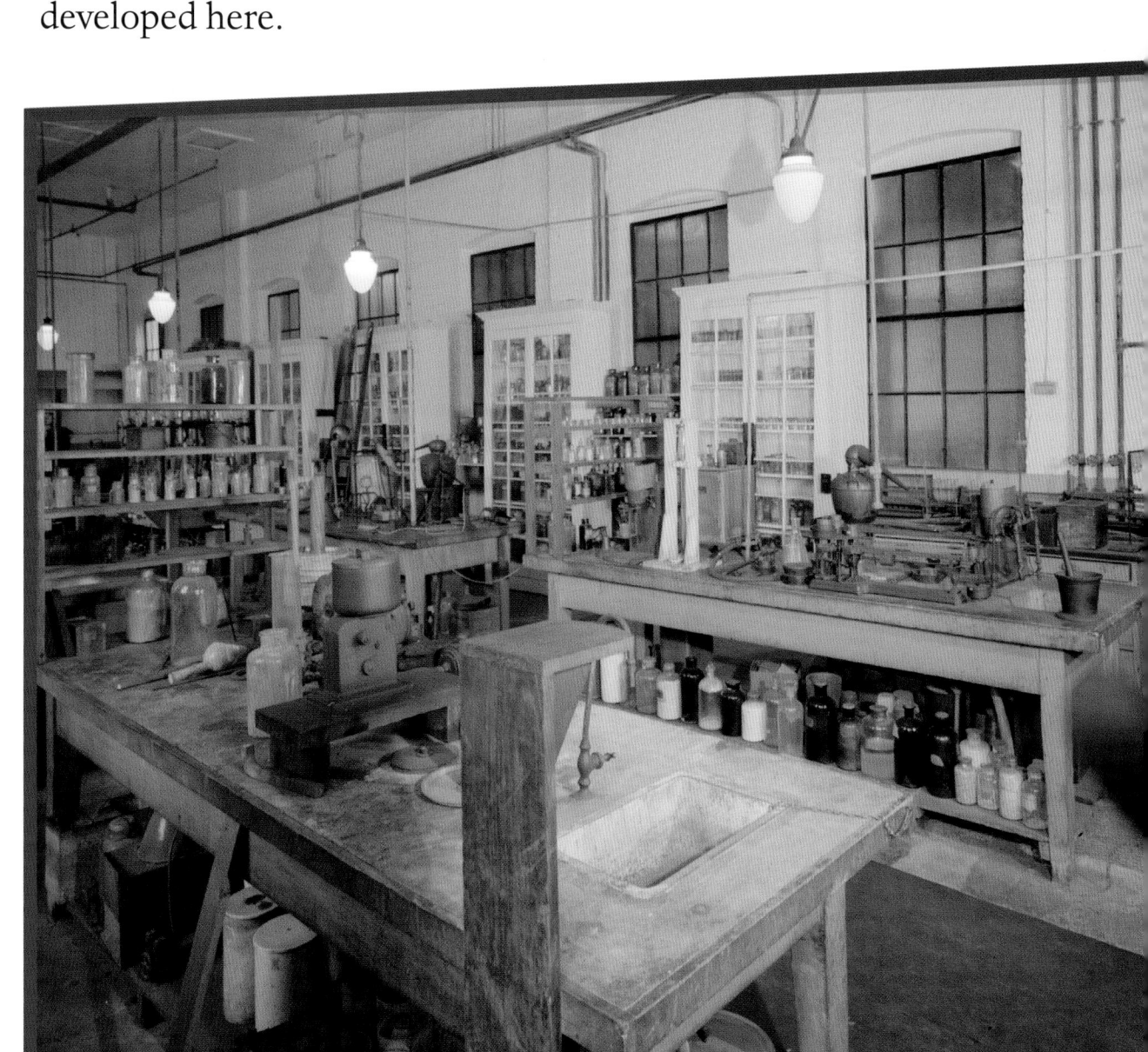

When Edison's West Orange Laboratory opened, he employed about 200 people there.

Motion pictures

In 1894, Edison's team invented a very early motion-picture machine called the Kinetoscope. Edison didn't think there was much of a future for motion pictures and he didn't file international patents. This meant that inventors overseas could copy and improve his ideas. That is exactly what they did. In France, the Lumière brothers patented the hugely successful cinématographe in 1895. They recorded and showed films to large audiences.

The Kinetoscope had a major drawback. It could be used by just one person at a time.

Edison wasn't to be outdone. He soon became involved with another **projector** called the Vitascope. Edison even built his own film studio at West Orange, to make motion pictures for the new projector.

In this publicity shot, Thomas Edison is shown holding a piece of film.

Into the 20th century

One of Edison's final successes was the nickel-iron battery, which was manufactured from 1903 to 1975.

During World War I, Edison became head of the Naval Consulting Board. This was a group of scientists and inventors who worked together to research and develop ideas that would help the United States in wartime.

Edison was a friend of the car manufacturer Henry Ford. In 1929 – the 50th anniversary of Edison's electric light bulb – Ford transported Edison's Menlo Park laboratory all the way to Dearborn, Michigan. He opened it as a museum.

Edison died two years later.

Edison's nickel-iron battery was used to power electric vehicles, like this one in 1910. The battery was rechargeable. Today, scientists are trying to improve Edison's battery so that it can be used in modern cars.

To celebrate the **golden jubilee** of the invention of Edison's light bulb, Henry Ford held a huge dinner in his honour. The guests included Marie Curie, Orville Wright, and US President Hoover.

After Edison

Thomas Alva Edison patented an astonishing 1,093 different inventions during his lifetime. Without him, communication, electric lighting, electricity supplies, sound recording, cinema, and many other advances in technology might have been very, very different. Edison's ideas changed millions of people's lives.

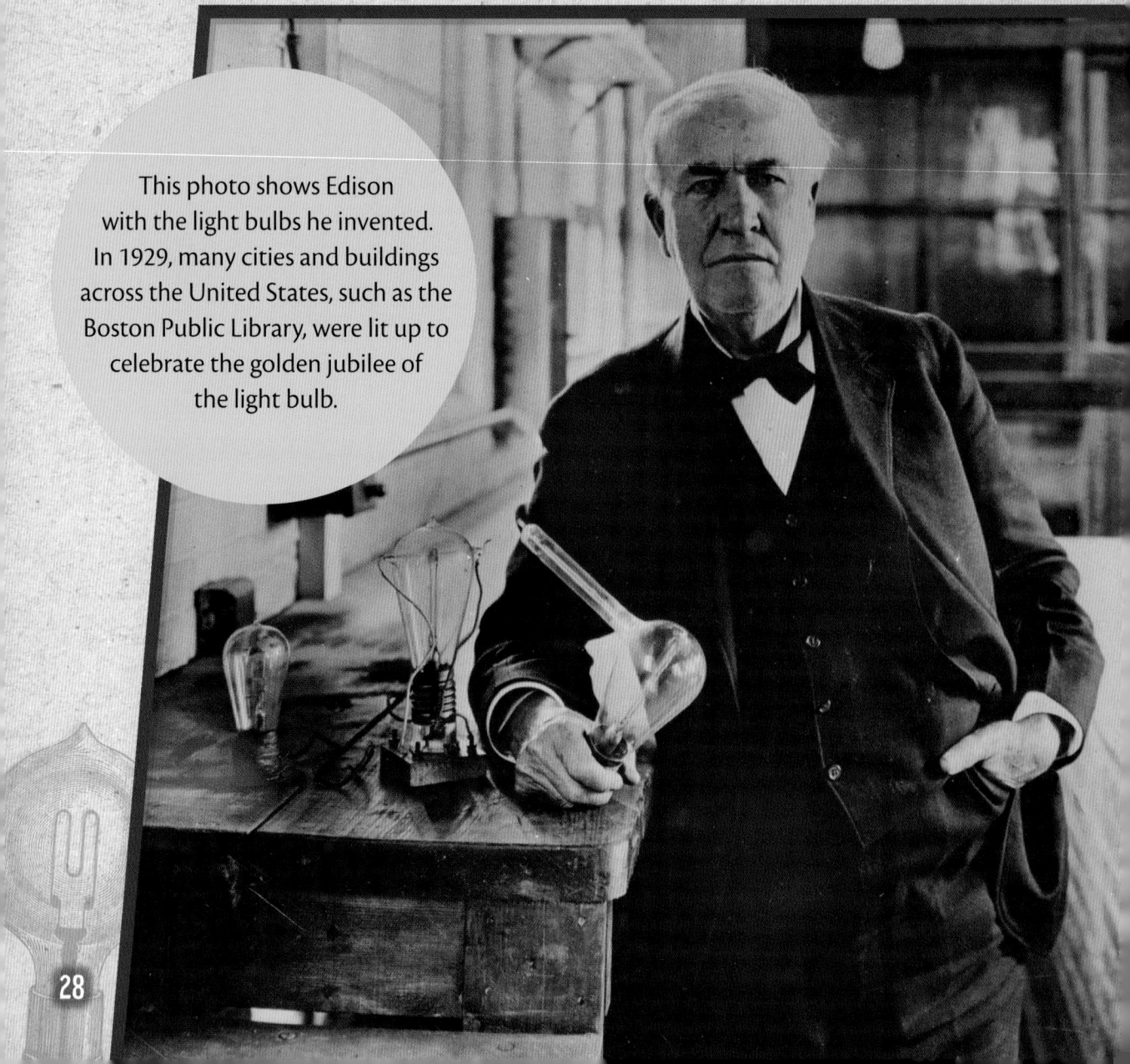

This photo shows Edison with the light bulbs he invented. In 1929, many cities and buildings across the United States, such as the Boston Public Library, were lit up to celebrate the golden jubilee of the light bulb.

Timeline

1847 Thomas Alva Edison is born in Milan, Ohio, USA, on 11 February

1859 Begins his first job on the railways

1863 Starts working as a telegraph operator

1869 Registers his first patent, for the electric vote recorder; becomes a full-time inventor and moves to New York City; makes improvements to the stock ticker

1871 Marries Mary Stilwell

1874 Invents the quadruplex telegraph

1876 Moves to Menlo Park, New Jersey

1877 Invents the phonograph

1879 Registers his first light bulb patent

1882 Opens the Pearl Street power station

1884 Mary Stilwell dies

1886 Edison marries Mina Miller

1887 Moves to West Orange, New Jersey

1900 Begins work on the nickel-iron rechargeable battery

1929 Celebrates Light's Golden Jubilee with Henry Ford

1931 Thomas Edison dies on 18 October, age 84

Glossary

alternating current (AC) a way of supplying electricity in which the electric current changes direction many times every second

ambitious wants to do well in life and work

device something made to do a particular job

digitally way of storing information as numbers so that it can be understood by a computer or other electronic device

direct current (DC) a way of supplying electricity in which the electric current travels in just one direction

golden jubilee celebration on the 50th anniversary of an event

industry type of business that has to do with making something

laboratory place where science experiments and research are carried out

licence permission to own, use, or do something

Morse code an alphabet in which each letter is expressed as a different combination of dots and dashes. For example, the letter A is . – and the letter B is – ... . These dots and dashes can be sent as signals along a telegraph wire.

motion picture old-fashioned name for a film

patent have a licence that shows that someone has invented something and nobody else can make it without paying the inventor a fee

phonograph very early machine that played sound and music

projector machine used to show film on a big screen

stock ticker machine that prints the prices of stocks onto a paper strip called ticker tape

stocks and shares small parts of a company or business that are owned by different people. Stocks and shares are bought and sold in a stock exchange.

telegraph system for sending messages along a wire as a series of electrical signals

vacuum space that has had all the air – including gases such as oxygen – removed

vinyl a type of plastic used to make records

Find out more

Books

The Illustrated Life of Thomas Edison (Charles River Editors, 2011)

Thomas Edison, Jan Adkins (Dorling Kindersley, 2009)

Websites

www.nps.gov/edis/forkids/index.htm
This is the website for Edison's home and laboratory in New Jersey.

www.show.me.uk/site/news/STO1493.html
This website includes information and a video about Edison's inventions.

Place to visit

Science Museum
Exhibition Road
South Kensington
London SW7 2DD
www.sciencemuseum.org.uk

Visit the Science Museum to see Edison's filament lamp.

Index